*WHAT IS THE REASON?*

# WHAT IS THE REASON?

## ?מהו הטעם

AN ANTHOLOGY OF QUESTIONS AND ANSWERS
ON THE JEWISH HOLIDAYS

### Volumes 4 & 5

# Chanukah & Purim

Compiled by
RABBI CHAIM PRESS

BLOCH PUBLISHING COMPANY

New York

*Printed in U.S.A.*

THIS BOOK IS DEDICATED TO THE MEMORY OF
MY BELOVED FATHER REV. JOSEPH PRESS who
took a great deal of pride in the achievements of his
children and grandchildren. His beloved memory is a living
inspiration in my life and in the lives of his entire family.


הספר הזה מוקדש
לזכר נשמת

אבי מורי ר׳ יותה זאב בר׳ גדליהו ע״ה

ת׳נ׳צ׳ב׳ה

בעז"ה

# PREFACE

Although it has been a few years since the publication of my last volume, I am hopeful that the publication of this latest work will serve as an impetus for me to complete the holiday set in the near future.

Recognition is due to the Young Israel of Fifth Avenue for its support through the good offices of Rabbi Israel Wohlgelernter, and to the Keren Hatorah Committee of Upper Manhattan for its assistance.

My thanks to Rabbi Haim Benoliel, Rabbi Marvin Luban, Rabbi Joseph Grunblatt and Rabbi Ephraim Wolf, for their encouragement, and to Rabbi Dr. Michael L. Munk for his constructive criticism and advice.

My appreciation to Gertrude Hirschler for reviewing the manuscripts, to Rabbi Berish Miller and Rabbi Eliyahu Safran for their editorial suggestions, and to Mr. Jack Strimban for his artwork and technical aid.

My special thanks to Mrs. Betty Marks of The Jewish Press for her cooperation.

And finally, my gratitude to the members of my family and to my friends for their encouragement.

Tishrei 5735

September 1974
                                                        C.P.

ואלה יעמדו על הברכה

| | |
|---|---|
| Yitzchok Braun | Lazar Margoshes |
| Nachum Dick | Eli Munk |
| Maurice Ehrman | Yehudah Munk |
| Leo Friedman | Jerome Muskal |
| Yitchok Gellis | Moshe Neuman |
| Peretz Gerstner | Shmuel Oelbaum |
| Shmuel Goldstein | Mottel Pinter |
| Ronald Greenwald | Yisroel Pressman |
| Baruch Greisman | Alan J. Rosenberg |
| Baruch Handler | Avrohom S. Rosenfeld |
| Shmuel Hertz | Pinchus Schaum |
| Naftali Hirsch | Marvin Schick |
| Baruch Katz | Menachem Shayovich |
| Yaakov Klass | Morton Shore |
| David Kleinbard | David Singer |
| Raphael Klugman | Pinchus Srebro |
| Chaim Y. Kofman | Moshe Y. Stern |

Mordechai Zuckerman

# TABLE OF CONTENTS 11

## INTRODUCTION

It is my pleasure to welcome the fourth and fifth volumes of "What is the Reason."

My good friend, Rabbi Chaim Press, has added Chanukah and Purim to his useful educational series. Like its predecessors, this book will be helpful to those seeking accurate information about the laws and customs of these unique days of our calendar. By the proven method of question and answer, the author has presented substantial material in an easy manner.

The references and notes allow the interested student to pursue his quest to the original sources.

This book is sent forth to add meaning to our observance of Chanukah and Purim. May it fulfill its goal.

Israel Wohlgelernter, Rabbi
Young Israel of Fifth Avenue
New York City

# QUESTIONS AND ANSWERS

# Chanukah

**QUESTION 1: What is the historical background of Chanukah and the origin of the *mitzvah* of kindling the Chanukah lights?**

**ANSWER:**  The Story of Chanukah is recorded in the Book of the Hasmoneans[1] and related in the Talmud.[2]

Approximately 2400 years ago, after the return to the Land of Israel from the Babylonian exile, the Children of Israel, by the edicts and cooperation of their Persian rulers, secured religious freedom. They were permitted to rebuild the ancient Temple that was destroyed by the Babylonians and they re-established their homeland on the sound foundation of Torah and Tradition.

However, when the Near-East was invaded and conquered by the Greeks under the leadership of Alexander the Great of Macedonia, many unfortunate changes began to take place. Hellenism started to make inroads in the Jewish way of life and Greek Culture began to replace the teachings of the Torah.

After the death of Alexander the Great and after the subsequent rule of the Ptolemies of Egypt, the Land of Israel had become a plaything in the political arena among the Greek generals who ruled the north and south. The Greek Seleucids who had conquered Syria then took control over the Jewish People in their Homeland. The most cruel and infamous among those who ruled over Syria at that time was Antiochus, who had issued many harsh decrees against the Jewish People. Religious practices,particularly circumcision, the observance of the Sabbath, the New Moon (and the Festivals) were prohibited under the threat of death. The Holy Temple was desecrated and defiled. Pagan Culture and Idolatry became the new order, and Hellenism became rampant throughout the land.

However, many loyal Jewish martyrs chose death and torture to the acceptance of the pagan idolatry and heathen cult of the Greeks. Yet others chose to revolt against the oppression in spite of their being weak and few in number against the strong and vast armies of the Greeks. Mattathias, the son of Jochanan, High Priest of the Holy Temple who with his valiant sons, among whom was Judah the Maccabean, were victorious over the hosts of their enemy with the help of the Almighty.

After the safety of their people was secured, the Hasmoneans turned their minds to rededicate and restore the Temple. When they came to light the Temple's Menorah (Candelabrum), they found only one cruse of undefiled oil bearing the seal of the High Priest. It contained no more than one day's supply of oil, but by a miracle of G-d the light burned for eight full days.

In the year that followed, those eight days were designated as a Festival of Thanksgiving, on which the *Hallel* (Psalms 113-118) is recited.

According to the Midrash[3], the twenty-fifth day of Kislev, the first day of Chanukah, was also the day when the *Mishkan*, the Tabernacle in the days of Moses, had been completed. At that time, G-d postponed the dedication of the Sanctuary until the month of Nissan, the month in which our Patriarch Isaac had been born. Generations later, the Midrash relates, G-d made amends for this slight by having the miracle of Chanukah occur during the month of Kislev.

Another Midrash[4] tells us that in the days of Moses, the chieftains of the Twelve Tribes of Israel brought sacrifices; each one was assigned a day for his offering. The Tribe of Levi, however, was omitted. To console the Levites for this omission, G-d commanded Moses to tell Aaron that his descendants would be given the privelege of lighting the Menorah when the Second Temple would be rededicated in the days of Hasmoneans.[5]

## QUESTION 2: What is the meaning of the term Chanukah?

**ANSWER:** Chanukah in Hebrew, denotes "dedication" such as when sacred objects were dedicated to Divine Service. In this instance it refers to the act of dedication performed by the Hasmonean Priests when the Temple was desecrated by the hordes of pagans who had invaded the Land of Israel. "Chanukah" then denotes the rededication of the holy altar and the Temple.[1]

## QUESTION 3: Why did the miracle of Chanukah last for eight days?

**ANSWERS:** 1. According to Biblical law (Numbers 19:11)[1] anyone coming in direct contact with a dead body becomes impure for a period of seven days. Accordingly, the Hasmonean Priests having become impure by contact with the dead in battle were not permitted to prepare new oil for Temple use until after seven days. After performing their ritual immersion for purification, they needed one additional day to prepare new oil. Hence eight days were needed until the new supply of pure oil was ready.[2]

2. The source of the fresh supply of oil was in the territory of the Tribe of Asher which was a four-day journey from Jerusalem. An additional four days was needed for its return. Hence it took eight days till the new supply of oil reached the Temple in Jerusalem.[3]

**QUESTION 4:** **Since there was sufficient oil to last for one full day, why is Chanukah celebrated for eight days and not just seven days?**[1]
**Note: The following are some of the various opinions as to how the miracle of Chanukah occured.**

**ANSWERS:** 1. The miracle of Chanukah actually lasted for eight days since a small amount of oil remained unused even after the first day.[2]

2. The oil found in the cruse was divided into eight parts. Hence the miracle took place eight full days.

3. Although the oil had burned all night the cups of the Menorah were found still full every morning including the first.[3]

4. Even after the Priests had poured the oil from the cruse into the cups of the Menorah, the cruse remained full.[4]

5. The first day of Chanukah commemorates the miracle of the military victory of the Hasmoneans over the enemies of Israel.[5]

6. The very discovery of the cruse of pure oil was considered a miracle for were it not found, there would have been no miracle of Chanukah.[6]

In this connection the following parable is cited.

A wealthy merchant travelled to market in the city with eight bags of golden coins. On the way he was robbed of all the bags except one, which the robbers overlooked.

Arriving at his destination, the man immediately hired a search party to find the robbers and vowed that if the L'rd would help him regain his money, he would donate one-tenth of it to charity.

To his great joy and relief, his prayers were answered.

When the administrators of charities came to the merchant to request the promised donation, the merchant argued that the tithe he had pledged applied only to the seven bags that had been stolen, and not to the eighth bag, which had gone unnoticed by the robbers.

To this, the administrators of charities replied that the tithe included the eighth bag, too, since it was only thanks to its contents that the merchant was able to hire the search party which recovered the other seven bags.

So it is with the miracle of Chanukah. Had the cruse not been found on the first day, there would have been no light at all. Accordingly, the first day of Chanukah is no less a part of the miracle than the other seven.[7]

**QUESTION   5: According  to  Talmudic  law[1],  the regulations persuant to ritual purity are suspended if the majority of the Jewish People is in a state of defilement. Why, then, was it so important to use only ritually pure oil for the kindling of the Temple lights?**

**ANSWERS:** 1. Pure oil was used as *Hiddur Mitzvah*—in order to beautify and elevate the observance over and above the strict letter of the law, as a recognition of G-d's love for Israel which he demonstrated with the salvation of His people.[2]

2. The rededication of the Temple was to mark a new beginning, an overt return of the Holy Presence to Its dwelling place.

Under the circumstances, ritually impure oil would have been unacceptable.[3]

**QUESTION 6: Since the major festivals are observed for one extra day in the Diaspora, why is Chanukah not celebrated for nine days instead of eight?**

**ANSWERS:** 1. Unlike the other major festivals of the Jewish Calendar, which are based upon Biblical law, Chanukah is observed as a Rabbinical ordinance. The Rabbis decided not to add an additional day of observance for Chanukah.[1]

2. To kindle nine lights would interfere with the symbolism basic to the practice of kindling eight lights to correspond to the eight days that the lights burned in the Temple.[2]

**QUESTION 7: Why can the first day of Chanukah never fall on a Tuesday?**

**ANSWER:** The fact is due to the specific arrangement in our Calendar by which the First Day of Rosh Hashanah can never be on a Sunday, a Wednesday or a Friday. (See Vol. 1. Q. 14.)[1]

**QUESTION 8: Unlike the other festivals, including Purim, Chanukah is not discussed in the Mishnah. Why not?**

**ANSWER:** This omission represents a protest by Rabbi Judah the Prince, the Compiler of the Mishnah who was a member of the Tribe of Judah and a direct descendant of King David, against the assumption of the kingship by the Hasmoneans of the Tribe of Levi, contrary to Jacob's promise to the Tribe of Judah (Gen. 49;10).[1]

**QUESTION 9: Why is the paragraph beginning with *Al Hanisim* ("For the miracles . . .") placed after the paragraph in the Amidah beginning with *Modim* ("We give thanks . . .")?**

**ANSWER:** As both texts serve the sole purpose of expressions of thanksgiving they are most appropriately placed together to constitute one whole as is the case also on Purim. (See Vol. 5).[1]

**QUESTION 10: It is an established rule[1] that if someone inadvertently omitted to recite *Al Hanisim* in the *Amidah* or in the Grace after Meals, he need not repeat the prayer. Why is this so?**

**ANSWER:** Because the paragraph beginning with *Al Hanisim* refers to a festival which is post-Biblical, established by Rabbinic ordinance, rather than of Biblical origin; hence it is not considered to be an integral part of the prayers.[1]

**QUESTION 11: Any kind of oil (or even candles) may be used for the kindling of the Chanukah lights, yet olive oil is traditionally preferable. Why is this so?**

**ANSWERS:** 1. The Menorah in the Holy Temple had to be
                       lit by no other oil than olive oil as is stated in
the Torah, (Exodus 27;20).[1]

2. While other kinds of oil and candles also
give clear and steady light, olive oil is preferable since the
miracle of Chanukah was performed with olive oil.[2]

**QUESTION 12: What is the additional function of the**
                          ***shamash* or "servant" light besides**
                          **kindling the other Chanukah lights?**

**ANSWER:**   The Talmud[1] states that in addition to being
                       used to kindle the other lights, the *shamash*
serves as a reminder of the prohibition against deriving any
personal use or pleasure from the Chanukah lights. If, by
some chance, pleasure is derived from the lights, it can be
said that it did not come from the actual Chanukah lights
but from the *shamash* light which is not subject to the
prohibition. (See Question 13).[2]

**QUESTION 13: But why is it foribdden to make use of**
                          **Chanukah lights for any personal**
                          **pleasure?**

**ANSWERS:** 1. To indicate that the Chanukah lights—
                       regardless of whether they are candles or
wicks saturated with oil—are not to act as ordinary lamps
just to impart physical light but have the higher function of
spiritual enhancement, proclaiming the miracle of
Chanukah.[1]

2. The Chanukah Menorah in the synagogues
or at home was meant to stand in place of the Menorah in

the Holy Temple in Jerusalem. Now, the oil used for the Candelabrum in the Temple was sacred and could not be used for any other purpose. Moreover, the Candelabrum in the Temple was situated within the sacred premises of the Temple where no profane use was made of the holy light.[2]

**QUESTION 14: As the *mitzvah* of kindling the Chanukah lights is derived not of Biblical origin but is a Rabbinic Ordinance, (See Question 6 Answer 1.), why, then, is the blessing phrased as follows: "Who hast sanctified us by His commandments and *commanded us* to kindle the Chanukah lights," implying that this *mitzvah* too has been commanded by G-d Himself?**

**ANSWER:**   Granted that the kindling of Chanukah lights as such is a Rabbinic ordinance, yet the Talmud[1] affirms that it is the Torah which commands us to comply implicitly with all the laws, decrees and ordinances enacted by the Sages (Deut. 17:17). Accordingly, when we kindle the Chanukah lights we are complying with the will of G-d.[2]

**QUESTION 15: What is the actual wording of the blessing over the Chanukah lights?**

**ANSWER:**   According to some versions it is "Lehadlik Ner Shel Chanukah"(To kindle the light of Chanukah"). Others omit "shel"—implying that the Chanukah lights are not to be used for personal pleasure (See Question 13), unlike the blessing over the Sabbath candles since they are meant to be enjoyed for themselves.[1]

**QUESTION 16:  At what hour of the evening should the Chanukah lights be kindled, and why?**

**ANSWER:**   According to many Authorities,[1] the Menorah should be lit when the stars begin to appear, and should continue to burn for at least half an hour into the night. This is considered the best time for *Pirsume Nissa,* the "public proclamation of the miracle," for this is the hour when the streets are usually crowded.[2]

**QUESTION 17:  What is the practice of the *Mehadrin Min Hamehadrin* ( — the most scrupulous) with regard to the kindling of the Chanukah lights?**

**ANSWER:**  According to the strict law[1] one light is to be lit by the head of each household on every night of Chanukah. The practice of the *Mehadrin* is to have a light lit by every male member of the family, but the *Mehadrin Min Hamehadrin* start with one light on the first night of Chanukah and add one more light on each of the following nights, i.e. two for the second night and three for the third night, etc. We follow the practice of the *Mehadrin Min Hamedhadrin.*[2]

**QUESTION 18:  Why is the kindling of the Chanukah lights different from other *mitzvoth* in that we follow the practice of the most scrupulous?**

**ANSWERS:** 1. Some Authorities[1] maintain that the supply of oil found in the Temple would have been sufficient for eight days without the necessity of a miracle if the wicks used for the Temple Candelabrum were made thin. However, for the sake of *Hiddur Mitzvah* (enhancing the performance over and above the ordinary requirement), the wicks of the Menorah were made thick to impart a larger and brighter light, (owing to the fact that thick wicks require much more oil than thin ones). This decision on the part of the priests necessitated the miracle, (to make the supply of oil last eight days). Mindful that *Hiddur Mitzvah* brought the miracle to pass in those days, we therefore go beyond the ordinary requirement of the law and follow the practice of the *Mehadrin Min Hamehadrin,* (See Question 5 Answer 1).

2. Another opinion[2] has it that this is our way of emulating the pious zeal of the High Priest who was in office at the time of the rededication. According to this view, the fact that the cruse of pure "beaten" oil found in the Temple bore the seal of the High Priest instead of that of the Keeper of the Oils—as was the usual practice for oil set aside for Temple purposes—indicates that the High Priest had originally intended the oil for use in his daily meal offering (*Minchath Chavitim*) (Lev. 6:12). As distinct from the oil used for the Menorah lights, Talmudic law did not specify "beaten" pure olive oil for the meal offering; ordinary olive oil would have been sufficient. It seems, that the High Priest went beyond the letter of the law and took only "beaten" pure olive oil even for his meal offerings. For surely had not the High Priest been of the *"Mehadrin"* but used just ordinary oil for the daily meal offerings, no oil would then have been found fit for the Menorah. In remembrance of the good that came from the *Hiddur Mitzvah* by the High Priest, we follow this practice and we are not content with the ordinary requirement.

**QUESTION 19:** **Since women are exempt from those positive precepts whose performance is subject to a fixed and definite time, why are they required to join in the observance of the *mitzvah* of kindling the Chanukah lights?**

**ANSWERS:** 1. The Talmud[1] states that women are required to participate in the observance of the kindling of the Chanukah lights, because they were directly affected by the miracle. Some Authorities[2] explain that this refers to the ending of the outrageous and cruel acts of immorality which the women were subjected to by the pagan invaders and their rulers.

2. As related in the Midrash[3], a miracle was performed through the help of a woman, Judith, the daughter of Jochanan, the High Priest. Her courage delivered her people from death. Judith was a beautiful woman and decided to use her charms to entice the Greek leader Holofernes. She fed him cheese to make him thirsty and wine to put him in a deep sleep. She then severed his head and brought it back to Jerusalem and displayed it before the enemy soldiers. The death of their leader caused them to panic and they beat a hasty retreat. (See Answer to Question 33).

Accordingly, women are also obligated to participate in the observance of Chanukah.[4]

**QUESTION 20:** **It is customary not to do any work in the house while the Chanukah lights are burning, and this custom is observed particularly by women. But why is this so?**

**ANSWER:** The custom to refrain from work while the
Chanukah lights are burning is to avoid the
possibility of transgressing the prohibition against the use
of Chanukah lights for personal purposes. This might
happen when the lights of the house suddenly go out, in
which case the Chanukah lights would be used to continue
work that was being done. The custom is observed primarily by women because it was a woman, Judith, who helped
to bring about the deliverance of her people (See Question
19, Answer 2).[1]

**QUESTION 21:** What is the source and special
significance of the recital which
follows the kindling of the Chanukah
lights and begins with *Haneroth
Halalu* ("These lights which we kindle
. . .")?

**ANSWER:** This text is found in the Talmud[1] and con-
sisted originally of thirty-six words (not including the title). This number of thirty-six is to bring to
mind the total number of lights kindled on the eight nights
of Chanukah (not including the shamash light).[2]

**QUESTION 22:** Since everyone is to participate in the
kindling of the Chanukah lights at
home (as previously stated), why then
are they kindled also in the synagogue?

**ANSWERS:** 1. The kindling of the Chanukah lights in
places of public prayer constitutes the sanc-
tification of the Name of G-d in public, thus proclaiming
the miracle of Chanukah to wider audiences than in
private homes. This is especially important today when we

no longer kindle the Chanukah lights outside our homes as was originally the custom in earlier days.[1]

2. It was also remarked that as the miracle of the Chanukah lights took place in the Holy Temple we celebrate that event also in the synagogues which are our Sanctuaries in miniature (*Mikdash Me-at* [2]).

3. As the kindling of the Chanukah lights is obligatory upon each and everyone in the community and as some may not be versed in the wording of the blessings and their order, it was deemed necessary to perform this *mitzvah* also in the synagogue and places of public prayer to acquaint the people with the proper procedure.[3]

4. It has also been suggested that Chanukah lights are kindled in the synagogue for the benefit of visitors who are away from home and have no chance to kindle the lights themselves or to watch them being kindled elsewhere.

In fact it was for the same reason that the *Kiddush* on Friday nights, and Festival nights is also recited in the synagogue, though the *Kiddush* over wine was intended for the home.[4]

**QUESTION 23:** **It is customary in some communities to kindle the Chanukah lights in the synagogue not only in the evening but also in the morning (without the blessings). What is the origin of this practice?**

**ANSWER:** To satisfy the requirements of those Authorities[1] who maintain that the lights in the Menorah of the Holy Temple, would have to be rekindled in the morning if they were extinguished during the night.

**QUESTION 24:  Why is the *Hallel* recited in its entirety on each of the eight days of Chanukah? (See Vol. 3 Question 24.)**

**ANSWERS:** 1. Each day of Chanukah is considered in the Talmud[1] as a festival in its own right, as the miracle of the cruse of oil recurred on each of the eight days of Chanukah; hence all the days of Chanukah are alike for the recital of *Hallel*.

2. And again, each day of Chanukah is distinct from the other days by virtue of the changing number of lights kindled on that day, just as each day of Succoth is distinct from the others by virtue of the changing number of sacrifices offered on each day.[2]

3. A further reason was advanced on account of the Torah readings for the eight days of Chanukah which are accounts of the sacrifices offered by the princes of the Twelve Tribes of Israel at the dedication of the Tabernacle in the wilderness. Each day of Chanukah is accordingly to be viewed as the particular festival of the tribe whose Prince offered his sacrifice on such a day. Now, each of the Princes surely recited the entire *Hallel* when he brought his sacrifices at the dedication of the Tabernacle, so we too recite the entire *Hallel* throughout all the eight days of Chanukah.[3]

**QUESTION 25:  On Chanukah only half *Kaddish* is recited by the Cantor after *Hallel*, unlike the practice on the Festivals and Rosh Chodesh, when the complete *Kaddish* is recited. Why the difference?**

**ANSWER:** The "full" *Kaddish* is recited only at the completion of a Service. On Festivals and Rosh

Chodesh, the Morning Service is followed by a *Mussaf* (Additional) Service, and since no *Mussaf* Service is held on Chanukah (See Question 29), the Kaddish that follows Shacharith is only "half" *Kaddish*. The full *Kaddish* is then recited at the very end of the Morning Service.[1]

## QUESTION 26: What is the Torah reading for the eight days of Chanukah and what is the reason for the selection?

**ANSWER:** The Talmud[1] states that the Torah portion for Chanukah consists of the Biblical account (Numbers 7:1-8:4) of the dedication of the Tabernacle and the offerings brought by the tribal Princes of Israel on that occasion. The Sages chose this account of an earlier dedication as the most fitting way to mark the observance of Chanukah, which commemorates the rededication of the Temple in Jerusalem.[2] Tradition[3] tells us that when Moses descended from Mount Sinai on the tenth of Tishrei —the Day of Atonement, (See Vols. 1&2), he brought the good tidings to the Children of Israel that the sinful act of worshipping the Golden Calf had been forgiven them by the grace of G-d, and that they were requested to erect a Sanctuary to the glory of G-d. The work was in fact done within two months and on the twenty fifth day of Kislev, was complete for consecration. This dedication was however deferred by Divine order until the first day of Nissan, the month in which Isaac had been born (to indicate that the dedication of the Altar presupposes the dedication of man to do the will of his Maker, and sacrifice himself to the glory of G-d of which Isaac is the historical symbol). To compensate for this slight to the month of Kislev, G-d promised that Kislev would receive its due centuries later, when the Hasmoneans would re-dedicate the Holy Temple in Jerusalem and the miracle of Chanukah would take place.

Accordingly, it is only proper that the account of that earlier dedication be read in the synagogue on this festival. (See Answer to Question 1).[4]

## QUESTION 27: Why do some congregations begin (on the First Day of Chanukah), the Torah reading with the Priestly Blessings, (Number 6:22-27)?

**ANSWER:** To honor the Hasmoneans, who were Priests.[1]

## QUESTION 28: Why is there no Haftorah reading for each day of Chanukah?

**ANSWER:** The Sages generally added a Haftorah to the Scriptual readings on days such as on Sabbaths and on those Festivals where work is forbidden and the congregation has time for a longer service. Since work is permitted on Chanukah it was felt that the synagogue service should not be lengthened by a Hafotrah reading.[1]

## QUESTION 29: Why is there no *Mussaf* (Additional) Service on Chanukah?

**ANSWER:** The *Mussaf* Service was instituted only for those days which were marked by "additional" festival offerings in the Temple in Jerusalem.[1] After the fall of the Temple, these sacrifices were replaced with the *Mussaf* Service in accordance with the words of Hosea (14:3) "We will render for bullocks the offering of our lips." Since Chanukah was instituted in the post-Biblical era, its observance was never marked by any sacrifices, and hence does not call for a *Mussaf* Service. (See Question 25).[2]

**QUESTION 30: What is the practice with regard to the kindling of the Chanukah lights on Sabbath eve?**

**ANSWER:** It is maintained by most Authorities[1] that the Chanukah lights are to be kindled prior to the Sabbath candles, i.e. approximatley twenty minutes before sundown, for once the Sabbath candles have been lit, the household has "officially" inaugurated the Sabbath, when no kindling of lights is to take place. In order to make sure that despite such an early kindling, the Chanukah lights will burn at least half an hour after nightfall i.e. the appearance of stars, sufficient oil or longer candles are to be used for the Menorah on Sabbath eve.[2]

**QUESTION 31: What are the special Haftorah readings for the Sabbath of Chanukah?**

**ANSWER:** Acccording to the Talmud[1], the Haftorah reading for the first Sabbath of Chanukah deals with the vision of the Menorah mentioned in Chapter 4 of the Book of Zechariah. When the week of Chanukah includes two Sabbaths, the Haftorah reading for the second Sabbath is the account of Solomon's Menorah in the First Book of Kings.[2]

**QUESTION 32: What is the practice as to the order of kindling Chanukah lights at the conclusion of the Sabbath i.e. whether it precedes the recital of *Havdalah* or not?**

**ANSWER:** According to most opinions[1], the kindling of the lights in the synagogue should precede the recital of *Havdalah*, in order to prolong the Sabbath outgoing by delaying the *Havdalah*, which officially inaugurates the workday week. Moreover, the kindling of the Chanukah lights, which publicly proclaims the miracle of Chanukah, should take place as early as possible, although *Havdalah* ordinarily takes preference, since it is recited more frequently.

Another opinion[2] advocates this procedure for home observance too, since the lights will be kindled in the home after the recital of *Havdalah* in the synagogue but before the recital of *Havdalah* at home. Still others [3] hold the reverse . . . i.e. that the Chanukah lights be kindled at home *after* the *Havdalah*. The *Havdalah* takes preference in the order since it is recited more frequently. Some more recent Authorities[4] consider either way acceptable.

## QUESTION 33:  Why is it customary to eat dairy dishes on Chanukah?

**ANSWER:**  Because Judith[1] fed cheese to the Greek Holefernes, which resulted in his death and the salvation of her people. (See Question 19 Answer 2).[2]

## QUESTION 34:  Why is it customary to eat foods fried in oil (such as "latkes") on Chanukah?

**ANSWER:**  To recall the miracle of the oil in the Temple.[1]

## QUESTION 35:  Why is it considered proper to partake of a festive meal on Chanukah?

**ANSWER:**  To commemorate the two historic events that occurred; namely, the dedication of the Tabernacle in the wilderness and the rededication of the

Temple in Jerusalem after the victory of the Maccabees. It was felt that a festive meal would serve to enhance the spiritual rejoicing with which Chanukah should be observed. (See Question 36).[1]

**QUESTION 36: Although it is considered proper to partake of a festival meal on Chanukah, the practice has not been set down as a specific *mitzvah*. On Purim, on the other hand, the partaking of a festive meal is mandatory. Why?**

**ANSWERS:** 1. Purim commemorates the miraculous rescue of the Jews from physical extermination, while Chanukah, commemorates the victory of the Torah, symbolized by the miracle of the Chanukah lights. Accordingly, it seems logical that the celebration of Purim should place much greater emphasis on physical delights, i.e. a feast or banquet, than that of Chanukah which is primarily a festival of spiritual rejoicing.[1]

Chanukah marks the defeat of the enemies of Israel who sought to suppress Judaism by decreeing that Greek idolatry be embraced and the Jewish religion abolished, thus commemorating the spiritual survival of the Jewish people. Purim on the other hand commemorates the defeat of a plan for the extermination of all Jews. Therefore on Purim the emphasis is on physical pleasures i.e. food and drink, and on Chanukah it is on spiritual rejoicing as expressed by the kindling of the lights, prayers and services of thanksgiving (and the study of the Torah).[2]

2. The main transgression committed by the Jews in the time of Purim was that they derived pleasure from the feasts of Ahasuerus. (See Vol. 5). Thus, G-d decreed that those bodies that enjoyed forbidden drink be destroyed. Accordingly, the physical salvation of the Jewish people is sufficient reason to celebrate the festival with feasting. The decree against the Jews in the time of Chanukah came as a result of the people's laxity in the sacrificial services. The decree of Antiochus was indeed measure for measure in that he brought to a halt the communal sacrifices of the Temple and caused the cessation of the kindling of the Menorah lights by defilement. When G-d saw the repentence and devotion of the people to restore the Temple, He wrought the miracle of the Chanukah lights through the Hasmoneans who were priests and in charge of the Temple Services. Since the destruction of the Temple, prayer is the substitute for the Temple Services; hence we celebrate Chanukah with prayer, praise and thanksgiving, and not with a feast or banquet.[3]

**QUESTION 37: What is the origin of the observance of the tenth day of Tebeth (Assarah BeTeveth) as a day of fasting and penitence?**

**ANSWER:** The sad events that occurred on the tenth day of Tebeth is recorded in II Kings 25:1, Jeremiah 52:12 and Ezekiel 24:2. The armies of King Nebuchadnezzar laid seige to Jerusalem. The seige ended with the destruction of the First Temple and the First Exile.[1]

**QUESTION 38: According to Jewish law, fasting on a Friday is not permissable (See Vol. 5**

**Question 6). Why then do we fast on *Assarah BeTeveth* even when it occurs on a Friday?**

**ANSWER:** This fast day is an exception since the passage describing the sad historical events of the day specifically states (Ezekiel 24:2) "On this very day"; hence fasting on Assarah BeTeveth is observed even on a Friday.[1]

**QUESTION 39: What is the origin and significance of the New Year of Trees (Chamishah Assar Bishevat or Tu Bishevat) observed on the fifteenth day of Shevat?**

**ANSWER:** As explained in the Talmud[1], this is the time of year when most of the rains have ceased in the Land of Israel, and the sap has already risen in the trees, thus introducing a new beginning which has become known as the "New Year of the Trees."

The fifteenth day of Shevat therefore marks the start of a new year in the computation of *Ma'aser* (the tithe), which everyone had to set aside and to give to the Levites, as explained in Numbers 18:21, and Deuteronomy 14:22. This was done every year except on the Sabbatical year of the *Shemitah* cycle, (when the field was left to lie fallow) as explained in Leviticus 25:3. This tithe was known as *Ma'aser Rishon* or "First Tithe".

On the first, second, fourth and fifth year of the cycle, an additional tithe known as *Ma'aser Sheni* (the "Second Tithe") had to be set aside and brought to Jerusalem to be used exclusively there. In the third and sixth years of the same cycle this *Ma'aser Sheni* was replaced by *Ma'aser Ani*, a tithe which was given to the poor. Fruits that blossomed during the interval between the first of Tishrei and the fifteenth of Shevat of the third and sixth years were considered as the fruits of the previous year and were not subject to *Ma'aser Ani* but to the laws of *Ma'aser Sheni* (of the second and fifth years).[2]

It is customary on *Tu Bishevat* to eat fruit grown in the Land of Israel and to recite the blessing of *She-hecheyanu* over the new fruit.[3] In the land of Israel it is customary to plant new saplings on that day.

### QUESTION 40: What are the "Four Special Sabbath Portions" read in the synagogue and what is their significance? And what are their respective Haftorah readings?

**ANSWER:** *Parshat Shekolim* (Exodus 30:11-16) deals with the half-shekel *(Machatzis Hashekel)* coins first used in the census of the Jewish people, and the money was used to cover the cost of public sacrifices. The Talmud[1] explains that on the first day of Adar announcements were made requesting these contributions. This Torah portion is appropriately read on the Sabbath introducing Rosh Chodesh Adar.

The related Haftorah is from II Kings, Chapters 11 and 12, a portion containing an account of the repairs made in the Holy Temple, paid for by the funds collected from the people for this purpose.[2]

*Parshat Zachor* (Deuteronomy 25:17-19) contains the command to the Children of Israel to remember the Amalekites and their cruel attack on them after they left Egypt. It is read on the Sabbath preceding Purim since Haman, who sought to kill the Jews was of Amalekite descent. (See Vol. 5).[3]

The Haftorah is from I Samuel, Chapter 15, which tells of the episode between the Prophet Samuel and Agag, King of the Amalekites.

*Parshat Parah* (Numbers 19) deals with the "red heifer" *(Parah Adumah),* whose ashes, when mixed with spring water and sprinkled on a person, removed impurity caused by contact with a dead body.[4] It is read prior to the Festival of Passover, when purity was required before the people could sacrifice the Pascal lamb.

The Haftorah is from Chapter 36 of the Book of Ezekiel in which the L'rd tells Israel, "I will sprinkle pure water upon you and you shall become clean" (36:25). It precedes Parshat Hachodesh because it deals with the purity of Israel (as stated in the Jerusalem Talmud[5]).

*Parshat Hachodesh* (Exodus 12:1-20) is read on the Sabbath introducing the New Month of Nissan, and describes the month of Nissan as the first month of the Hebrew year and tells of the command to offer the Pascal sacrifice.[6]

The Haftorah is taken from Chapters 45 and 46 of the Book of Ezekiel, and it deals with the Pascal sacrifice.

# Purim

## QUESTION 1: What is the origin and significance of the Festival of Purim?

**ANSWER:** With the destruction of the First Temple and the extinction of the kingdom of Judah, our forefathers were exiled into Babylonia. Before long the Persians conquered Babylonia and the surrounding countries and granted a certain amount of autonomy to their Jewish subjects, so much so, that Cyrus, King of Persia, permitted the Jews to return to their homeland, rebuild their Temple and cities, and re-establish their religious and national life.

In the course of this period Ahasuerus came to power and ruled over 127 provinces.

As related in the *"Megillah"* ("Book of Esther")[1] his Prime Minister Haman, decided to annihilate all the Jews within those provinces. Haman cast "lots" to select the actual month and day when he would carry out his evil intentions. Hence the name "Purim," which means "lots"—cast by Haman. The lots indicated the month of Adar, and the 13th day thereof. Vashti, meanwhile, King Ahaseurus' wife was executed for refusing to attend the king's banquet, and a Jewess, Esther, was chosen from among the fairest in his empire to be the new queen. Mordecai, her relative, who was a member of the Sanhedrin (Jewish High Court), also enjoyed a high position in the King's service. Advised and instructed by him, Esther interceded on behalf of her people and exposed Haman's plot to the king. In a rage of anger the King ordered Haman to be hanged and allowed the Jews to defend themselves against anyone who sought to destroy them.

The fourteenth day of Adar, (the day after the date set by Haman,) was fixed by the Sages for the Festival of Purim.[2]

**QUESTION 2:** **In a leap year of the Jewish calendar, when there are two months of Adar, the first Adar being the twelfth month and the second Adar being the thirteenth month, Purim is celebrated in Adar II. But judging by verses in the Megillah (3:7 and 9:1) where the twelfth month is mentioned in connection with the events of Purim, it would be more plausable to have its celebration on the twelfth month in any year. Why then celebrate Purim on the 13th month in a leap year?**

**ANSWER:** This matter occupied the attention of our Sages in the Talmud[1] who declared that the Festival of Passover celebrating the redemption of our people from the house of bondage in Egypt was the prototype of miracles such as Purim. Accordingly the two celebrations even though they refer to different periods in our history, must be taken together and brought as close as possible to each other. Hence, Purim must be celebrated in the month that precedes the month of Nissan, even in a leap year.[2]

**QUESTION 3:** **Purim can never fall on a Monday, a Wednesday or a Sabbath. Why not?**

**ANSWER:** Regarding these days it has been pointed out that on account of Calendar arrangements and considerations the fourteenth day of Adar I or II could not be on these two days, just as Yom Kippur can never be on a Sunday, Tuesday or Friday. (See Q. 14, Vol. 1.).[1]

**QUESTION 4: Since most other holidays are celebrated for one additional day in the Diaspora, (See Vol. 1 Q. 15) why is Purim not celebrated for two days?**

**ANSWERS:** 1. Since the observance of Purim is based on Rabbinic rather than Biblical law, the Sages decided not to add an additional day of observance for Purim. (See Vol. 4 Q. 6).[1]

2. In the case of Purim there is a further consideration based upon the phrase in the Megillah (9:27) . . . "and it should not fail that they would keep these days according to the appointed time thereof, every year . . ." This passage could also be taken to imply that it should not be put off or repeated on a subsequent day. Hence Purim is not to be observed on a subsequent day.[2]

**QUESTION 5: The Eve of Purim is observed as Taanith Esther, (The Fast of Esther). What is the reason?**

**ANSWERS:** 1. Some authorities[1] find the reason in that Esther had fasted and declared a public fast day as recorded in the Megillah (4:16).

2. However many authorities[2] attribute the reason to the commemoration of the fast observed in the past by Jewish warriors who went out to battle. In fact the Talmud[3] states that when the Children of Israel led by Joshua fought against the Amalekites (Ex. 17) and Moses stood in prayer to invoke Divine Mercy in the hour of peril, they observed a strict fast.

We accordingly observe the Eve of Purim as a public fast day to impress upon us that the Almighty is near to all those who are in distress and engage in fasting and repentance.

**QUESTION 6: When Purim falls on a Sunday, the Fast of Esther is observed on the previous Thursday. Why not on Friday? (It obviously cannot be observed on the Sabbath since partaking of the Sabbath meals is mandatory.)**

**ANSWERS:** 1. It was realized that fasting on a Friday would not be in keeping with the honor due to the Sabbath day. Firstly, the food for the Sabbath meals would have to be prepared at a time when one would be unable to taste it and ascertain whether it was properly cooked and seasoned.[1] Moreover, it would mean that we would have to start the Sabbath day while in a state of fasting and depression.[2]

2. And again, the many Selichoth compositions (penitential prayers) which are to be recited on fast days would take away too much time from a day which is used mainly for making adequate preparations for the Sabbath day.[3]

**QUESTION 7: Why then is the Fast of Esther observed on Thursday and not put off to Sunday as is the case of other Fast days?**

**ANSWERS:** 1. The fast of Esther cannot be put off till the following Sunday as this is the day of Purim, which cannot be observed while fasting, for it is a day of celebration and feasting.[1]

2. And again, the other fast days (which commemorate the tragic destruction of the Holy Temple and Exile), must not be observed on the previous Thursday for the reason stated in the Talmud,[2] that tragic events should not be commemorated prior to the exact days of their actual occurrence. The Fast of Esther on the other hand, does not commemorate a tragedy as such, but is a memorial to the acts of courage and heroism shown by the Jews who were saved by the Grace of G-d.[3]

**QUESTION 8: What is the origin of the custom to contribute three *half-shekal* coins (or half-dollars) before reading the Megillah? (See Vol. 4., Q. 40.)**

**ANSWER:** The custom of contributing three *half shekalim* on Purim is based on the fact that the term in the Torah (Ex. 30:13), dealing with the mitzvah of the *half-shekel* is mentioned three times, which was obligatory in the days of old when we had our Sanctuary, but is now observed as a symbolic act to recall the practices of our forefathers.[1]

**QUESTION 9: Since on Purim we publicly read the story of the miracle of Purim from the Megillah, why don't we read the Megillah of Antiochus on Chanukah, which describes the events and the miracles of the Hasmonean struggle? (See Vol. 4).**

**ANSWER:** The Megillah of Antiochus is not a part of our Sacred Writings. It is just a historical record of the miraculous events of Chanukah. In fact the Talmud[1] states that it was only by the special request of Queen

Esther that the Sages decided to include the Megillah of Esther among the Sacred Writings with the express proviso that it is to be the last in our sacred Canon.

Therefore since the events of Chanukah took place at a later time in our history, a Megillah dealing with Chanukah could not be included in the Sacred Writings.[2]

**QUESTION 10:** The Megillah is unscrolled and folded back like a letter before it is read, which is not the case with the other scrolls. Why the difference?

**ANSWERS:** 1. This is to bring to mind the *"iggereth"* (letter) (9:29) the official letter dispatched by Mordecai and Esther proclaiming the deliverence of their people from the evil plot of Haman and proclaiming the Feast of Purim to be observed by all Jews in every generation![1]

2. By unraveling the Megillah and folding it back, the miracle of the day is more publicized.[2]

**QUESTION 11:** The Divine Name of G-d is not mentioned even once in the Megillah, which of course is not the case in any other of our scriptures. What is the reason for this omission?

**ANSWERS:** 1. According to Midrashic sources[1], Mordecai had indeed intended to mention the name of G-d in the official letter which he dispatched to his people throughout the 127 provinces of the Persian Empire proclaiming the Festival of Purim. However, he did not mention it specifically for he felt that it might fall into the hands of heathens who might substitute the Holy Name with the name of their idols.[2]

2. According to the Talmud,[3] the Sages refrained from using the Name of G-d in the Megillah as such "letters" are likely to be thrown away; thus causing degredation to the Holy Name. When at a later date the scroll was included into the Sacred Writings, it was still considered proper to retain the original wording of the document set forth by Mordecai and Esther.[4]

3. It has been suggested by Rabbi Samson Raphael Hirsch[5] ( 19th Cent.) that the Holy Name was purposely not mentioned in the Megillah to teach us that the hand of G-d is ever-present in the history of man, even when we fail to see it openly, as the case in the events which lead to the miracle of Purim.

**QUESTION 12:** **Prior to the reading of the Megillah we recite the blessing *al mikra Megillah* (concerning the reading of the Megillah), while prior to sounding of the shofar, we recite the blessing *lishmoa kol shofar* (to hear the sound of the shofar). (See Vol. 1). Why is there no reference to the hearing of the reading of the Megillah?**

**ANSWER:** In the case of the Megillah, the mitzvah is not just to hear the reading but the act of reading itself, but in the case of the shofar, the mitzvah is not fulfilled by the act of blowing the shofar but by the hearing of the sound of the shofar.[1]

**QUESTION 13:** **In view of the fact that women are exempt from those positive precepts
whose observance is dependent on a
fixed time, why are they obligated to
hear the Megillah read on Purim?**

**ANSWERS:** 1. Because the women, too, were delivered
from the evil decree of Haman.[1]

2. Because it was a woman—Queen Esther
who played a vital role in the miracle of Purim.[2]

**QUESTION 14:** **It is the general practice to have the
Megillah read in the synagogue rather
than at home (where it is read only in
exceptional cases). Now since the
Megillah is an obligation on each and
every individual, why then is the synagogue preferred for this purpose?**

**ANSWER:** As the principle purpose of reading the
Megillah is to publicize the miracle of Purim
(Pirsume Nissa), the Synagogue which is the public place
for prayers is preferred. (See Prov. 14:28)[1]

**QUESTION 15:** **When listening to the reading of the
Megillah we will observe that four
verses (2:5, 8:15, 8:16 and 10:3) are also
read aloud by the congregation. What
is the reason for this practice?**

**ANSWER:** It is suggested that this practice was in-
troduced to keep the attention of the congregation (especially the young) on the reading of the
Megillah.
It was also thought that such a practice would lead to a

detailed description of the miraculous events of Purim. As to the specific choice of these verses, it is of course to pay a special tribute to Mordecai who together with Esther, played vital roles in the miraculous events of Purim.[1]

**QUESTION 16:** We will also observe that in the reading of the passages of the Megillah, the naming of the ten sons of Haman (9:7-9:9) is done in one breath without any interruptions whatsoever. What is the reason for this practice?

**ANSWER:** The Talmud[1] states that this practice is an indication that they were all hanged together, simultaneously. Even as Haman their father, sought to annihilate all the Jews at one time, so was he punished, and instead his sons were all hanged together at one and the same time. The preceding verse (9:6) which says, "In Shushan the Jews slew and destroyed five hundred men," is joined and also read aloud by the congregation for the reason that the five hundred men had all been under the command of the ten sons of Haman, each son being in charge of a company of fifty and were executed together with them.[2]

**QUESTION 17:** When the name of Haman is mentioned during the Megillah reading, noises are made to blot out the name. What is the reason?

**ANSWERS:** 1. It is related in the Talmud[1] that whenever Rabbi Judah the Prince, (in the course of his studies of the Megillah) reached the name of Haman, he would say "cursed be Haman and his sons," as it is written ... "and the name of the wicked shall be obliterated"

(Prov. 10:7) Accordingly, it became a custom especially among children to inscribe the name of Haman on sticks or pieces of stones which are beaten together so as to have his name erased in a literal sense.

As time went on, this practice gave rise to the present custom of making noises whenever Haman's name is mentioned and thus blot out his name.[2]

2. It was moreover suggested that this custom is based on the verse (Ex. 17:14), "For I will utterly blot out the remembrance of Amalek from under the Heaven," (See also Deut. 25:19). The name Haman was to be blotted out, as he was a descendant and actual prototype of Amalek.[3]

3. And again it is stated in the Midrash[4] that the last Hebrew letter of each of the first three words of the Biblical passage (Deut. 25:2) "Then it shall be if the wicked man deserves to be beaten", spell out the name of *Haman*, indicating that this name is to be beaten, as that of the wicked.[5]

**QUESTION 18:** **In the Megillah the first Hebrew letter (vav) in the name (Vay'zatha) the last of the ten sons of Haman listed in the Megillah (9:10) is larger than the other letters in the Megillah. What is the reason?**

**ANSWER:** It is mentioned in the Talmud[1] that this enlarged letter (vav) was to indicate that the sons of Haman were hanged on gallows, tall enough so they could be suspended in a long vertical line—one above the other.

For this reason there is a practice in some congregations to have the reading of this letter in particular, drawn out.[2]

## QUESTION 19: In the Megillah the Hebrew letter (Tav) in the word *Vatichtov* "and (Esther) wrote" (9:29), is larger than the other letters. What is the reason?

**ANSWER:** This enlarged letter is to indicate that just as the "tav" is the last letter in the Hebrew alphabet so is the Megillah of Esther the last record of miracles to be included in the Sacred Writings as stated by the Sages.[1]

## QUESTION 20: In the liturgy of Purim a special *piyut* (poem) is recited for every blessing during the repetion of the Amidah, not so with the blessing of *Eth Zemach Dovid*, "The offspring of David." What is the reason for this omission?

**ANSWERS:** 1. This blessing of the Amidah is a fervent supplication for the salvation of our people to be achieved through the restoration of the Kingdom and Dynasty of the House of David. Now the salvation achieved by the miracle of Purim was not at all connected with the House of David, but rather with that of the House of King Saul of the Tribe of Benjamin who preceded David on the throne of Israel and whose reign was temporary. When we pray for the permanent restoration of the Kingdom of David and the coming of the Messiah it is not considered proper to include a poem or praise of King Saul, namely of Esther and Mordecai of the Benjamite tribe whose ancestry was of the royal House of Saul.[1]

2. While most of the battles in Biblical history were fought and won by the dynasty of the House of David, which belonged to the Tribe of Judah (Gen. 49:8), the son of Jacob and Leah, the struggle against Amalek and his

descendants (including Haman) was waged by the descendants of Jacob and Rachel, i.e. the Tribe of Benjamin, including Mordecai.

Accordingly, the Liturgists omitted the piyut on the blessing refering to the House of David, in deference to Mordecai and Tribe of Benjamin.[2]

## QUESTION 21: Hallel is not recited on Purim, whereas on Chanukah it is recited (See Vol. 4). What is the reason for the difference?

**ANSWER:** It is stated in the Talmud[1] that Hallel which is an integral part of our Thanksgiving Prayers is to be recited only for those miracles that occurred in the Land of Israel. Hence, the difference between the Festival of Chanukah is that Chanukah celebrates miracles wrought in the Land of Israel, and Purim celebrates miracles wrought outside the Land of Israel.

As to the question why do we recite Hallel on Passover which also commemorates miracles that took place outside the Land of Israel, it is answered in the Talmud that the previous rule which limits Hallel to miracles wrought in the Land of Israel refers only to such miracles that took place after the conquest of the Land of Israel in the days of Joshua but not to any miracle that preceded that time. Hence the miracles of the Exodus are not subject to this qualification.[2]

2. It is stated in the Talmud[3] also that the Festival of Purim does not reqire the recital of Hallel for the very reading of the Megillah is the best form of Hallel and Thanksgiving.

3. The Talmud[4] gives yet another reason. Hallel as we know it starts with Psalm 113 which at the very

outset refers to our people as "the servants of the L'rd."
Now by the miracles of the Exodus celebrated on Passover
our people secured full freedom from under the yoke of such
oppressors as the Pharaohs and they had indeed become
the servants of the L'rd, by achieving absolute independence. But in the case of Purim, although saved from
annihilation, the Jewish people did not as yet enjoy
freedom and independence, but still remained in exile under the domination of foreign rulers. Even after the events
of Purim we remained the slaves of Ahasuerus, in which
case our people could hardly be referred to as only "the servants of the L'rd." Hence the Hallel is not to be recited on
the day of Purim.

## QUESTION 22: What is the Torah reading for Purim morning and why was it chosen?

**ANSWER:**   The Talmud[1] states that the last nine verses
of Chapter 17 of Exodus is the text of the
Torah reading for Purim morning, as it tells of the first
savage attack of the Amalekites against the people after
their exodus from Egypt. As Haman is a descendant of
Amalek, the reading is quite appropriate.

It is indeed noteworthy that the selection of this text
which consists of only nine verses is the only exception to
the general rule that any Torah reading in the synagogue
must consist of a minimum of ten verses. The reason for
this exception is because of the great significance of this
selected reading though brief in the number of verses, is
complete as a unit and historical record.[2]

**QUESTION 23: Why is there no Haftorah reading for Purim?**

**ANSWER:** The answer given to Q. 28 in Vol. 4 applies here too.[1]

**QUESTION 24: The She-hecheyanu blessing is recited prior to the reading of the Megillah on Purim Eve. Why then repeat it on Purim Morning?**

**ANSWERS:** 1. It has been stated by some authorities[1] that the blessings of *She-hecheyanu* is repeated in the morning because the morning reading constitutes the main mitzvah of the day.

2. There are special mitzvoth of Purim such as the sending of food portions to friends, gifts to the poor and the festive Purim feast which must be performed during the daytime and which are not provided with any particular blessing.

Hence the *She-hecheyanu* blessing is to be recited also in the morning to include the performance of those duties.

It is accordingly necessary to keep in mind the performance of those special duties at the time when the *She-hecheyanu* blessing is recited in the morning.[2]

**QUESTION 25: It is the general practice to wear Tefillin when the Megillah is read on Purim morning. What is the reason?**

**ANSWER:** According to the Sages,[1] the word *viykar* (and honor) (8:16), refers to the Tefillin. Accordingly it is therefore appropriate to wear the Tefillin when the Megillah is read.[2]

**QUESTION 26:** **A *Brith* (Circumcision) is usually performed in the morning after the completion of the entire Morning Service. Why then is it the practice to perform a *Brith* before the reading of the Megillah on Purim morning?**

**ANSWERS:** 1. According to the Sages,[1] the word *"sasson"* (joy) refers to the joy which accompanies a *Brith.* Hence it is appropriate to perform the *Brith* prior to the Megillah reading.[2]

2. So that the passage in the Megillah (8:16) "the Jews had light and gladness and joy and honor," can apply to the new infant as well as he enters into the covenant of the Jewish people.[3]

**QUESTION 27:** **After the Megillah reading in the evening there is a special prayer beginning with *"asher he-ni"* (Who has annuled) which is recited by the entire congregation. However after the Megillah reading in the morning, this prayer is not recited. What is the reason for this omission?**

**ANSWER:** In the morning when we recite many piyutim (liturgical poems) during the Repetition of the Amidah (which of course is not the case with the Evening Service), any additional prayer to the same effect would be redundant.[1]

**QUESTION 28:** **From the Megillah (9:22) we learn of the mitzvah to send gifts of food (*Mishloach Manoth*) on Purim. Why then do we not recite an appropriate blessing for this mitzvah?**

**ANSWERS:** 1. Although the performance of a mitzvah, whether commanded by the Torah or by the Sages, requires the recital of a suitable blessing, nevertheless, it is restricted to such acts which are carried out completely by the one who is performing the mitzvah.

In the case of the mitzvah of sending gifts to friends the performance is incomplete until the very moment the gift is willingly accepted by the friend to whom it was sent. Up to that time, no complete mitzvah was performed. Hence there is no recital of a blessing over the mere act of sending the gift.[1]

2. It has further been suggested that no blessings were prepared for the act of this mitzvah on the basis of an exact and literal translation of the term "re-ehu" (friend) which occurs in the verse in the Megillah (9:22), prescribing the duty of its performance. The term "friend" as such has a connnotation to mean a "true" friend. Since it is almost impossible to ascertain the degree of sincerity and friendship, it could be that the mitzvah was not actually performed properly. Accordingly, such a blessing, using the Name of the Al-mighty, may be in vain.[2]

2. A further theory was advanced to the effect that blessings were instituted exclusively for such acts of a mitzvah which would never have been done except as a behest command by the Torah or Sages. The very wording "Who has commanded us" indicates that the act is being done exclusively for the sake of heaven. It is therefore understood that the acts which might have been done as good

deeds such as the distribution of charity which would not have a blessing recited for them.

The mitzvah of sending gifts surely falls into this category, for which a blessing is not appropriate.[3]

**QUESTION 29:** **Among the special features of the day is the Purim Masquerade. What is the origin of this custom?**

**ANSWERS:** 1. It is our firm belief that all that takes place in the history of men and nations is decreed by G-d.

In discussing the events of the impending doom facing the Children of Israel in the days of Mordecai and Esther, the Sages[1] explained that the Almighty never intended that such a decree be carried out. It was a pretense and a necessary move in the mysterious ways of G-d, Ruler of all history, to have the Children of Israel of that day believe that a calamity of such magnitude was going to happen. Hence the popular custom to use all sorts of masks and disguises which are donned on Purim today, to demonstrate the pretentious move of the hand of G-d.[2]

2. Some[3] suggest that the custom is based upon a play on the word *"astir"* (Deut. 31:18), "I will hide."Now the Talmud[4] remarks that the Hebrew word *"astir"* has the same consonant letters as the name "Esther." Hence the practice of hiding one's face by means of masks, has become popular.

3. Another authority[5] suggests that it recalls the disguise of those gentiles who pretended to become Jews after seeing that the Jewish people had overcome their enemies who tried to destroy them.

**QUESTION    30: Why is it considered mandatory to partake of a festive meal on Purim, when it is not obligatory to do so on Chanukah?**

**ANSWER:**  See Vol. 4 Answer to Question 36.[1]

**QUESTION 31: The Purim feast is held during the daytime (usually in the afternoon before sundown). What is the reason?**

**ANSWER:**  The practice is in keeping with the literal implication of the verse in the Megillah (9:22), "that they should make them *days* of feasting and gladness."

The feast is usually held in the afternoon rather than in the morning because of the practical considerations i.e. the hours taken up with the longer morning service, which includes the reading of the Megillah, and the sending of food portions *(mishloach manoth)* and giving gifts to the poor and needy *(matanoth la'evyonim).*[1]

**QUESTION 32: It is a custom to imbibe wine and/or other intoxicating drinks at the Purim banquet and during the day. What is the reason?**

**ANSWER:**  The Talmud[1] remarks that wine (and other such intoxicating drinks) played a vital role in the events of Purim. Reference in the Megillah is made to the wine so lavishly used by King Ahasuerus at his royal parties which brought about the execution of Vashti, his queen, which in turn led to Esther becoming the Queen of Persia.

It is also stated that the downfall of Haman which resulted in the rescue of our people at this critical moment

was also due to the wine and other intoxicating drinks
which Queen Esther served so liberally at the banquet she
tendered for the King and Haman his Prime Minister. She
wisely used the feast as a most opportune time to plead for
the lives of her people.[2]

**QUESTION 33:  The day that follows Purim—that is
the fifteenth of Adar (Adar II in a leap
year) is known in our calendar as
Shushan Purim and is observed as a
semi-holiday in many ways. What is
the reason for this?**

**ANSWER:**  The origin of Shushan Purim is found in the
Megillah itself (9:21-22) which clearly states
that in Shushan, (the capital of the Persian Empire where
the evil influence of Haman still persisted among certain
groups which were hostile to the Jews), the Jews had to defend themselves also on the 14th day (for which special per-
mission of the king was granted), unlike their brethren in
the other parts of the empire who had to defend themselves
only on the previous day i.e. the 13th day of Adar and tak-
ing rest on the 14th day declaring it a day of joy and
gladness.

The Jews of Shushan however were not able to overcome
their enemies until the 15th day at which time they
celebrated and rejoiced.

To perpetuate this historical fact, it was then resolved
and enacted by the Sages[1] that in the future, Purim was to be
celebrated on the 15th day and not the 14th for the Jews in
Shushan and such other walled cities, with rejoicing and the
reading of the Megillah.

**QUESTION 34:** **According to Talmudic[1] law, Shushan Purim is to be observed in Shushan and all cities that were surrounded by a wall at the time of Joshua, when the Children of Israel entered the Promised Land. Why is this so?**

**ANSWER:** This qualifying condition regarding walled cities is based on the principle of honoring the Land of Israel and its cities, which lay in ruins in the days of Mordecai and Esther, as stated in the Jerusalem Talmud.[2]

# SOURCES AND FOOTNOTES

מקורות והערות

חנוכה

# SOURCES AND FOOTNOTES

## (מקורות והערות)

### Question 1

1. ע' מגילת תענית, מגילת אנטיכוס ס' החשמונאים, ע"ע ס' יוסיפון.
2. שבת כא.
3. מדרש רבה במדבר י"ג, ילקוט שמעוני (מלכים).
4. שם.
5. מדרש שם, ע' רמב"ן בהעלותך.

### Question 2

1. ע' מהרש"א שבת שם, ע' רש"י מגילה ל., וע' אור זרוע בשם אבי הנחל שגם כל כלי שרת נתחנכו, ובעל מור וקציעה ע"ש חנוך ההיכל וע' של"ה שחנוכה רומז לחנוכת העולם וע' בס' המועדים בהלכה.

### Question 3

1. ע' יבמות סא., ורמב"ם הל' טומאת מת פ"א ס' י"ב דגם עכו"ם מטמא טומאת מגע ומשא.
2. טור, ב"י.
3. ע' מאירי, ר"ן, אבודרהם, ע' רוקח.

### Question 4

1. זוהר, ע' רמב"ן תרומה ומג"א ש"ע או"ח ק"פ, וע' מאירי שבת שם, ב"י. (וע' מגילת תענית ובשאלתות „אפילו יום אחד" (או אלא יום אחד.)
2. ט"ז.
3. ב"י.
4. שם, וע' שלטי גבורים על המרדכי.
5. ע' מאירי, פרי חדש, ע' ברכי יוסף וע' בס' קדושת לו.
6. טור בשם שכנה"ג.

7. ס' קומץ מנחה. וע' בדרשות **חת"ם** סופר (מובא גם בס' נר למאה)
שנותן טעם לשבח שהי' די בשמן להדליק בפנים אבל לא בחוץ
(בגלל האויר) והיינו המשך—והדליקו נרות בחצרות קדשיך (ולא
בפנים בהיכל) על כן קבעו שמונת ימי חנוכה. וע' בעל העתים
ובערוך השלחן. ע"ע בשו"ת מור ואהלות שאם הי' עושים חנוכה
ז' ימים לא הי' ניכר בכל יום שהולכה כבית הלל וע' בס' ערבי נחל
ובתולדות יעקב יוסף המובאים בס' המועדים בהלכה — שהנס הי'
באמת ז' ימים והיום הח' הוא משום ספיקא דיומא (ע' ברכי יוסף).
וע' בס' שואל ומשיב ועוד מה שתירצו—להמנע מעשיית המנורה
של ז' קנים שעובר בלאו. וע' בס' אור תורה ועוד—שבלעה המנורה
מהשמן ונפחת . . . והי' נס שדלק כל הלילה וע' בשפת אמת שח'
ימים כנגד ח' ימים של סוכות . . . וע' מה שתירץ בס' מלוא העומר—
כולם מובאים בס' נר למאה וע"ע בס' נר מצוה למהר"ל שז' ימים
הוא טבע וח'—זה למעלה מן הטבע כמו אצל מילה ע"ש.

## Question 5

1. יומא ו: ועוד, ע' הרא"ם בביאורו לסמ"ג ע' פני יהושע וע' בהחכם
צבי. שבת שם—דטומאה הותרה בצבור.
2. שם.
3. ע' ד"ז בעלי תוס' שמיני, מהר"ל (ובשם מראה יחזקאל) וע' בחידושי
הרי"ם, ובס' חכמת שלמה על ש"ע או"ח הל' חנוכה, עי' בס' נר
למאה. וע' בשדי חמד מערכת חנוכה.

## Question 6

1. אבודרהם בשם בעל העיטור, ע' עטרת זקנים, וע' מנחת חינוך ש"א.
2. פר"ח—ויש עוד טעמים.

## Question 7

1. ע' שו"ע או"ח תכ"ח וע' שערי תשובה (מר חשון וכסלו מתחלפים
אם מלא אם חסר).

## Question 8

1. חתם סופר, ע' רמב"ן ויחי.

## Question 9

1. אבודרהם, ע' שבת שם.

## Question 10

1. ע' ש"ע או"ח תרפ"ב, ע' פמ"ג ומשנה ברורה שם.

## Question 11

1. ע' מדרכי, כל בו, מהרי"ל.
2. ע' ש"ע או"ח שם, ושער הציון ש"ע או"ח תרע"ג, ונוהגים גם להדליק
   בנר של שעוה—רמ"א. וע' מהר"ל בס' נר מצוה ומובא בעטרת זקנים
   שלא להדליק בנר של שעוה או חלב שלא מקרי נר רק אבוקה ופסול
   לנר חנוכה כי נר ואבוקה תרי מילי נינהו . . . וע"ע במחצית השקל
   שם.

## Question 12

1. שבת שם, וע' ש"ע או"ח שם.
2. שם, ע' רמ"א, מג"א, ששמים השמש גבוה משאר נרות וע' ט"ז
   (מהרי"ל)—שרמז על זה—שרפים עומדים ממעל לו (ל"ו נרות) וע'
   בס' לקוטי מהרי"ח.

## Question 13

1. רש"י, לבוש.
2. ר"ן, לבוש, ע' משנה ברורה ש"ע או"ח שם.

## Question 14

1. שבת שם.
2. אבודרהם.

## Question 15

1. ברכי יוסף, מג"א, שו"ע או"ח תרע"ו בשם מהרש"ל, מ"מ, של"ה, וע'
   האר"י ז"ל ובשם הגר"א. ויש עוד מנהגים.

## Question 16

1. (ע׳ רמב״ם). טור או״ח תרע״ב. וע׳ בבאור הלכה ובמשנה ברורה
. שמביא שיטות—שהזמן הוא מתחלת שקיעה ולא מסוף שקיעה.
2. מג״א, פר״ח, וע׳ משנה ברורה שם.

## Question 17

1. שבת שם.
2. המחבר (ב״י) פוסק כתוספות והרמ״א פוסק כהרמב״ם—וזה חידוש
שהספרדים נוהגים כתוס׳ והאשכנזים כרמב״ם וזה לא מצינו בשאר
מקומות (באר היטב), ע׳ ש״ע או״ח תרע״א, וע׳ בס׳ המועדים בהלכה.
ואשה אינה בכלל מהדרין ואם יש לה בעל אינה מדליקה דאשתו
כגופו — ע׳ א״ר בשם תשו׳ ש״א. מובא במשנה ברורה ובס׳ לקוטי
מהרי״ח, וע׳ בס׳ חידושי חתם סופר על מס׳ שבת — שנ״ל טעם
שנשים אינן מדליקות מפני שבתחלה תקנו להדליק בחוץ אז לא
נמצאה שום אשה שתצא להדליק שכבודה בת מלך פנימה — אע״ג
שמדליקים עכשו רק בפנים מ״מ מנהג הראשון לא זז ממקומו.

## Question 18

1. חידושי הרי״ם.
2. שם ועוד — וע׳ בס׳ נר למאה.

## Question 19

1. שבת כג.
2. רש״י, כל בו.
3. מדרש (מעשה) יהודית (וי״א שמעשה יהודית לא קרה בזמן החש־
מונאים) וע׳ כתובות ה.
4. כל בו שם.

## Question 20

1. מ״מ ועוד.

## Question 21

1. סופרים כ.
2. ע׳ טור, אבודרהם, לבוש, ע׳ מג״א בשם מהרש״ל, ע׳ מ״מ, מט״א
בשם פסקי הרא״ש וע׳ רוקח בשם מדרש רבה בראשית שהל״ו נרות
כנגד ל״ו שעות ששימש אור הגנוז לאדה״ר, וע׳ בס׳ בני יששכר,
וע׳ בס׳ לקוטי מהרי״ח.

## Question 22

1. ע׳ ש״ע או״ח תרע״א וב״י שם, וע׳ ריב״ש, וע׳ מה שמובא גם בס׳
המטעמים ועוד.
2. ע׳ עטרת זקנים בשם הרא״ש, כל בו ועוד.
3. ב״י, כל בו, וע׳ בס׳ טעמי המנהגים ומקורי הדינים.
4. ב״י, לבוש, כל בו, וע׳ שבלי הלקט.

## Question 23

1. ע׳ בס׳ אורחות חיים בשם שו״ת בנין שלמה — כדי לצאת דעת
הרמב״ם פ״ג הל׳ תמידים ומוספים.

## Question 24

1. ערכין י. (ע׳ שבת כא).
2. ב״י או״ח תרפ״ג בשם שבלי הלקט.
3. שם ע״ע אבודרהם.

## Question 25

1. ע׳ לבוש.

## Question 26

1. מגילה לא.
2. ע׳ לבוש.
3. פסיקתא, עיטור.
4. ע׳ רמב״ן בהעלותך.

## Question 27

1. טור, לבוש.

## Question 28

1. נועם מגדים מובא בס׳ טעמי המנהגים ומקורי הדינים הל׳ פורים.

## Question 29

1. ע׳ ברכות כו ::
2. ע׳ רש״י שם ועוד.

## Question 30

1. ע׳ ר״ן שבת, טור, ר״י, כל בו.
2. ע׳ ש״ע או״ח שם.

## Question 31

1. מגילה לא.
2. ע׳ טור וב״ח, וב״י מביא בשם הר״ן שאע״ג הנרות דשלמה קדימי
   אפ״ה עדיפי לן דזכרי׳ משום דנבואות עתיד נינהו.

## Question 32

1. ש״ע או״ח תרפ״א (המחבר).
2. רמ״א שם דכ״ש בביתו — מג״א, א״ר, והגר״א.
3. ע׳ ט״ז ובשם המהר״ל ותיו״ט ועוד, וע׳ בבאור הלכה שמביא הרבה שיטות בענין זה.
4. משנה ברורה דמסיק דעביד כמר עביד ודעביד כמר עביד.

## Question 33

1. מדרש (מעשה) יהודית שם.
2. כל בו, ר״ן — מובא ברמ״א ש״ע או״ח תר״ע.

## Question 34

1. ע׳ מג״א ובאר היטב על המנהג שנותנים כסף שקורין „חנוכה געלט״ (או מתנות) בחנוכה, וע׳ בס׳ חנוכת הבית ובס׳ המטעמים וע׳ בס׳ בני יששכר טעמו על מה שמשחקים בסביבון וע׳ בס׳ טעמי המנהגים ומקורי הדינים ועוד.

## Question 35

1. ע׳ רמ״א שם, וע׳ בס׳ המנהגים ובס׳ ערוך השלחן.

## Question 36

1. ט״ז.
2. לבוש.
3. ב״ח, ע׳ מס׳ מגילה.

## Question 37

1. ע׳ להלן

## Question 38

1.‎ ב"י הל' תענית. (וטעם דמתענים ביוה"כ שחל בשבת הוא גם משום
שנאמר „בעצם היום הזה").

## Question 39

1.‎ משנה ר"ה פ:א וע"ש י"ב.

2.‎ ע' רמב"ם.

3.‎ ע' ש"ע או"ח רכ"ה (ויש מנהגים שונים אם מברכים ברכת שהחיינו
קודם לברכת הפרי או אחרי . . . ע' משנה ברורה שם והטעמים).

## Question 40

1.‎ שקלים פ"י-י', ע' מגילה כט :.

2.‎ ע"ע ש"ע או"ח תרפ"ה ונושאי כלים שם.

3.‎ הרבה סוברים שקריאה זו מן התורה, ע' ת"כ, מגילה יח. תוס' שם
יז. ובברכות יג., ע' ש"ע שם מג"א, ערוך השלחן ומשנה ברורה.

4.‎ י"א שגם קריאה זו מן התורה אבל רוב שיטות סוברות דרבנן היא
אף שיש רמזים בתורה (דאסמכתות הן).

5.‎ להזהיר לישראל שיעשו הפסח בטהרה (וע' רש"י מגילה שם ובדין
היא שתקדים פ' החודש לפרה שבא' בניסן הוקם המשכן ובב'
נשרפה הפרה ומפני מה הקדימוה — שהיא טהרתן של כל ישראל
(ירושלמי מגילה פ"ג ה:ה) וי"א שגם פרשה זו מן התורה וע' תוס'
רי"ד חסיד (ברכות) וריטב"א (מגילה), וע"ע ש"ע או"ח שם.

6.‎ שם.

פורים

## Question 1

1. ע׳ מגילת אסתר.
2. מס׳ מגילה.

## Question 2

1. מגילה ז.
2. מהרי״ל, לבוש, ועוד.

## Question 3

1. ע״ש. וע״ע שם במס׳ מגילה עוד טעמים לשבת.

## Question 4

1. אבודרהם.
2. שם, וע׳ מגילה ב :, וע׳ ש״ע או״ח תרפ״ח.

## Question 5

1. ע׳ סופרים, ב״י בשם הרמב״ם וע׳ לבוש.
2. ע׳ רש״י, טור, רא״ש, ר״ן, ב״י — ש״ע או״ח תרפ״ו, וע׳ קצש״ע הל׳ מגילה.
3. מגילה יד :.

## Question 6

1. לבוש.
2. ע׳ טור, ר״ן ריש מגילה בשם תשובות הגאונים, ע׳ ערוך השלחן.
3. טור וש״ע או״ח הל׳ תענית.

## Question 7

1. מ״מ ועוד.
2. מגילה ה..
3. א״ז — מגילה וע׳ טעמו של הר״ן ריש מגילה, וע׳ בס׳ אוצר כל מנהגי ישורון.

## Question 8

1. רמ״א (ד״מ) ש״ע או״ח תרצ״ד.

## Question 9

1. מס' מגילה.
2. ספרים.

## Question 10

1. טור, ש"ע או"ח תר"ק, וט"ז, ב"ח שם ועוד.
2. שם, רמב"ם ועוד.

## Question 11

1. ע' מדרש רבה אסתר וע' פרקי דר"א.
2. ע' מהרי"ל, ט"ז בשם מרדכי.
3. ר"ה יח..
4. ס' אשכול.
5. כתביו, ומעין זה מובא מרב האי גאון וע' בסדור יעב"ץ מהאר"י ז"ל שיש הרבה שמות ה' הרמוזים במגילה. ויש עוד טעמים.

## Question 12

1. אבודרהם, לבוש, א"ר, ע' ש"ע או"ח תרצ"ב וע' מגילה יח.. וברכות ט"ו, ויש עוד טעמים.

## Question 13

1. רש"י מגילה.
2. תוס' שם.

## Question 14

1. ע' מגילה ה :. ע' רמב"ם ושאר ראשונים וע' ש"ע או"ח תר"ק.

## Question 15

1. אבודרהם בשם בעל משמרת המועדות וע' בס' התניא.

## Question 16

1. מגילה טז :.
2. וע' ט"ז בשם הרוקח — ובדיעבד אם הפסיק יצא — ע' רמ"א, וע' מ"מ בשם תוס' וע' בס' צפנת פענח שמצדיק מנהג הקהלות שאומרות עשרת בני המן בקול רם היום ואי אפשר להוציא אחר מדי נשימה. וע' בס' המועדים בהלכה.

## Question 17

1. ירושלמי מגילה, וע׳ יומא לח.. וע׳ מדרש רבה בראשית.
2. רמ״א.
3. ע״ש ועוד.
4. מדרש רבה אסתר.
5. ע׳ מהרי״ל, לבוש, מ״מ (וע׳ בס׳ מנהגי בית יעקב).

## Question 18

1. מגילה.
2. לבוש, וע׳ בס׳ תורה תמימה על מגילת אסתר.

## Question 19

1. ע׳ יומא כט.. וע׳ בס׳ כל מנהגי ישורון.

## Question 20

1. זרע קדש.
2. אגרא דפרקא וע׳ טעמו של היעב״ץ בסידורו וע׳ בס׳ טעמי המנהגים ומקורי הדינים.

## Question 21

1. ערכין י..
2. שם.
3. שם.
4. שם ויש עוד טעמים.

## Question 22

1. מגילה לז. ע׳ תוס׳ ורא״ש שם.
2. ע״ש וע׳ מגילה כג. וע׳ בס׳ טעמי המנהגים — קריאת התורה.

## Question 23

1. ע״ש.

## Question 24

1. טור בשם ר״ת והרא״ש ועוד, רמ״א ש״ע או״ח תרצ״ב.
2. מג״א בשם של״ה, ע׳ משנה ברורה שם, וי״א (ב״י) שאין מברכים שהחיינו בבקר.

## Question 25

1. מגילה טז:.
2. מ"מ, ס' מנהגים — מובא בבאר היטב — ש"ע או"ח תרצ"ג.

## Question 26

1. מגילה ז:, ע' ש"ע או"ח תרצ"ה.
2. מג"א ועוד.
3. ע' ש"ע או"ח שם, מהרי"ל מובא במחצית השקל, וע' דרכי משה.

## Question 27

1. מג"א בשם הלבוש, מובא גם בס' לקוטי מהרי"ח, וע' אבודרהם שמבאר התפילה כנגד אלה שנלחמו בעמלק.

## Question 28

1. ע' רמ"א ש"ע או"ח תרצ"ה וע' פמ"ג תרצ"ב.
2. ארחות חיים.
3. ע' שפת אמת ועוד.

## Question 29

1. מגילה טו:, וע' רמ"א ש"ע או"ח תרצ"ו, א"ר.
2. בני יששכר.
3. מובא בס' אוצר כל מנהגי ישורון.
4. חולין קלט:.
5. שפת אמת מובא בס' יינה של תורה.

## Question 30

1. ע"ש.

## Question 31

1. ס' מנהגים, ע' רמ"א ש"ע או"ח תרצ"ה וע' מגילה ה' וע' ט"ז, מג"א, באר היטב ועוד.

## Question 32

1. מס' מגילה.
2. אבודרהם ועוד. וע' בסדר היום טעמו, ע' רמב"ן וע' ר"ן בשם רבנו אפרים.

## Question 33

1. מס׳ מגילה, ירושלמי.

## Question 34

1. שם, וע׳ רע״ב ועוד.
2. שם.

נר הי נשמת אדם

(משלי כ:כז)

**In Loving Memory**

**ל ז כ ר   נ ש מ ו ת**

מורי ורבי הרב הג׳ ר׳ דוד קראנגלאס ז״ל
זקני ר׳ יצחק בר׳ יהודה גערשטנער ז״ל
גיסי ר׳ שמואל צבי בר׳ חיים זאב קאפס ז״ל
דודי ר׳ לוי בר׳ יונה רבינאוויץ ע״ה
החזן ר׳ שמרי׳ בר׳ ישראל הערמאן ע״ה
אחיני, הילד יונה זאב בן ר׳ יוסף ארי׳ פרעס ע״ה
ר׳ יהושע בר׳ משה שאר ע״ה
ר׳ דניאל יצחק משה בן הרב בן ציון שלמה לפידות ז״ל


הרה״ח ר׳ אברהם זישא ז״ל בן הרה״ח ר׳ יצחק מאיר הי״ד
זיסקינד
החבר אברהם בן החבר יואל קלוגמאן ז״ל
שהלך לעולמו ו׳ מנחם אב תש״י
הרב ר׳ יהודה בר׳ חיים יוסף דוב גלאצער ז״ל
ר׳ משה צבי בר׳ מרדכי הלוי קמינעצקי ע״ה
ר׳ חיים מרדכי בר׳ משה מוזעז ע״ה
ר׳ פרץ בר׳ יצחק שיינערמאן ז״ל
ר׳ ישראל בר׳ פסח יוסף אקערמאן ע״ה
ר׳ אהרן בר׳ דוד מארקאוויץ ע״ה
ר׳ יצחק בר׳ יונה קאפלאן ע״ה
ר׳ חנינא ליפע בת ר׳ נפתלי הירץ קץ ע״ה
ר׳ שמואל בר ישראל לעווענטאל ע״ה
ר׳ דוב בער בר׳ נחום קמזן ע״ה
ר׳ יהודה יצחק בר׳ משה נומאן ע״ה
תלמידי החבר משה בן החבר אורי שלום הלוי לימאן ז״ל


ת׳נ׳צ׳ב׳ה

לזכר נשמות

סבתי ה׳ בײלע בת ר׳ שאול מאיר גאלד ע״ה
סבתי ה׳ פריידא בת ר׳ חיים אליהו גערשטנער ע״ה
דודתי ה׳ פרומע ברכה בת שבע בת ר׳ יונה
רבינוויץ ע״ה
ה׳ לאה מלכה ברוידא בת הרב פסח דיסקינד ז״ל
ה׳ אסתר בת ר׳ יצחק ליב קץ ע״ה
ה׳ חי׳ פייגע בת ר׳ אהרן גלייך ע״ה
ה׳ רבקה מעניא בת רב ליב אליה וואלפיש ע״ה
ה׳ צירל בת ר׳ זעליג קמיניצקי ע״ה
ה׳ בלומע בת ר׳ חיים לעווענטאל ע״ה
ה׳ גאלדא רחל בת ר׳ ישראל מנחם סרברו ע״ה


ת׳נ׳צ׳ב׳ה